GRAVEL ROAD AHEAD

poems by

Sue Fagalde Lick

Finishing Line Press
Georgetown, Kentucky

# GRAVEL ROAD AHEAD

Copyright © 2019 by Sue Fagalde Lick
ISBN 978-1-64662-053-1 First Edition
All rights reserved under International and Pan-American Copyright Conventions.
No part of this book may be reproduced in any manner whatsoever without written permission from the publisher, except in the case of brief quotations embodied in critical articles and reviews.

ACKNOWLEDGMENTS

"Evening Meal," *Nexus*, July 1, 2009
"What He Saw," (previously "Vision"), published in 2010 *Write on the Sound* prize booklet as second place winner.
"Wifely Duty," *New Letters*, Summer 2016
"Empty Pockets," *Concord*, Vol. 3, 2011
"He'll Never Know," *Concord*, Vol. 4, 2012
"His Whisker," *Diverse Voices Quarterly*, June 2012

Publisher: Leah Maines
Editor: Christen Kincaid
Cover Art: Sue Fagalde Lick
Author Photo: Kristin Cole
Cover Design: Elizabeth Maines McCleavy

Printed in the USA on acid-free paper.
Order online: www.finishinglinepress.com
       also available on amazon.com

          Author inquiries and mail orders:
              Finishing Line Press
                P. O. Box 1626
           Georgetown, Kentucky 40324
                  U. S. A.

Table of Contents

One Week after the Diagnosis 1

Sundowning 2

Evening Meal 4

As the Fog Closes In 5

Must I Give This Up, Too? 6

Sleepwalking 7

Dementia Divorce 8

Coffee Stains 9

Vision 11

What a Feeling 12

Gravel Road Ahead 13

Not Staying 14

Friday Afternoon 15

Wifely Duty 16

Just another Day 17

Alzheimer's Activity 18

Memory Care 19

This, Too, Will Pass Away 20

Empty Pockets 21

Love Remains 22

I'm Your Wife 23

He'll Never Know 25

Keeping the Widow Warm 26

New Year's Day, Albany General, Room 204 27

Your Kiss in the Back of a Buick 28

His Whisker 29

Widow on the Road 30

Sister Alzheimer's Wife 31

ONE WEEK AFTER THE DIAGNOSIS

Walking the dog at sunset,
my husband takes the leash.
His shoulders hunched,
shoes crunching gravel,
he stares straight ahead
to the dimming before
total darkness comes.

Even now, words flee
like sparrows the instant
he reaches for them.
Names, dates, thoughts.
It's as if someone
turned off the lights.
He is blinded, lost.

I lead the way,
planning our dinner,
clinging to my lists,
while the dog pauses
to sniff a garter snake.
My man gently reaches out
to touch the red-striped skin.

Turning back, I watch.
When he stands up again,
I match my steps to his.
Left, then right, then left.
I reach for his fingers,
dry-skinned and cold,
and hold on as tight as I can.

SUNDOWNING

As I prepare to leave for class,
his new doctor's receptionist calls.
He answers. I'm busy trying to pour
spinach soup from a giant bowl
into the narrow mouth of a Thermos.

He keeps asking me questions:
What's our cell phone number,
what is our neighbor's last name,
what is her telephone number, where—
Stop! I don't have time for this.

"It's that new doctor. He wants me to--"
I grab the telephone out of his hand
to inform Michelle at the Alzheimer's clinic
that she's asking the man who can't remember
for all the things he can't remember.

I agree to a date I had planned
to get my teeth cleaned, and I promise
to bring his insurance card and co-payment.
I take down directions as the clock ticks past
the time I had planned to leave.

I close up my Thermos, grab a Coke,
zip my bulging briefcase closed. Waiting,
he hugs me tight, pressing my gold chain
hard against me through my shirt. "Sorry,"
he says. "I know you have too much to do."

His kiss fresh on my lips, I drive fast to town,
climb the stairs, sweating, my heart beating.
Thank God the classroom light is off.
My students are later than I am. I fill the board
with quotations in green, homework in red.

Three students show up, all sleepy and bored,
their homework half done. Why bother, I think,
for thirty-seven dollars a night, for the sake
of the three, as the old man asked the Lord.
I gulp my soup as they write me a poem.

After class, I drive into the sunset.
A diagonal red and purple line
bruises the moonless blue-black sky.
I turn the car toward the state park where
I ram a thumb of concrete hard.

Colors blending into gray,
lighthouse blinking to the north.
I circle stone benches, gazebo, rocks,
get back into the car. On the bridge,
a road worker waves his sign. Stop.

At home, the dog leaps for a cookie,
but the man whom I left behind is gone,
replaced by a cut-stringed puppet
slumped in his chair, TV on loud.
"Any news?" I ask him. "No," he says.

Butter uncovered, cabinet ajar,
phone off the hook on the table. Two
calls missed, says the Caller ID.
As the last glimmer of daylight disappears,
I eat three pieces of stale birthday cake.

EVENING MEAL

Warm dog nudges my leg.
I reach under the kitchen table,
blindly stroking the soft fur.
My dinner plate is empty.

The man eats slowly,
scrapes his knife across his dish,
piles half-chewed bloody gristle
beside potato peels and celery strings,
tosses tooth-grooved artichoke leaves
into a bowl that doesn't match.

Clock chimes 7 o'clock.
Darkness shrouds the windows:
cloth thrown over a birdcage.
Chandelier hangs, five moons
circling an incandescent sun.
Melting margarine, tarnished spoons.

He cuts, bites, chews, stops.
The dog groans, lowering her head.
She stares at me, brushes my knee,
listens for his fork to drop,
waits to pounce on gristle and blood.

AS THE FOG CLOSES IN

Honey, I want you to see
beyond tonight's TV shows
all the way to morning,
to tomorrow, to forever,
to dream what's possible
and even what's not.

But a cloud hangs
so close you see only
where you stand right now.
And me. You follow me.
You who wear the shadow
hang heavy on my back.

Carrying you is hard.
I can see forever,
but your dead weight
forces me to crawl
one inch at a time.
I cannot spread my wings.

The cloud is closing in.
You shout out now in fear
as it nullifies your soul.
I clutch your trembling hand.
At this moment, you know only
that you are not alone.

I wish you could know that
above the fog, heaven waits.
Oh, climb, reach for it.
Let me feel you finally
lifting off my back,
rising into the light,
then reaching down for me.

MUST I GIVE THIS UP, TOO?

You reach for me in bed.
I slide into your arms like a latch
falling into place. I wrap my legs
around your warm pajama'd limbs.
I rest my cheek against your skin.
I sigh. Home at last. But it doesn't
work. "Where are you?" you mumble,
fumbling for my face in the dark
until I find your hot, dry lips.
We kiss three times then, always three,
as if that were the secret code.
Then you pull away, your hand
brushing again my breast.
My body screams for more.

SLEEPWALKING

Your side of the bed springs empty.
I hear you slide along the wall.
Bang! You crash into the closet door.
My eyes snap open like window shades.
Your white tee shirt glows in the near-light
of clock-radio numbers and star-shine
as you turn toward the window, stumbling
over the dog dozing at the foot of the bed.

"Crap," I whisper, jumping up to grab you.
Your skin is hot and sweaty, your body
rigid as Madame Toussaud's wax models.
I spin you round to face the hallway door,
but you walk straight ahead toward your office.
"No." I turn you again. Melting man of wax,
are your eyes open? I can't see them in the dark.

Through the bathroom door at last.
Nightlight flickers yellow-orange.
"Thank you," you say and shut the door.
Back in bed, reclaiming the mangled sheets,
muttering, "Oh man" to the dog and to God,
I lie waiting, wondering. Are you peeing
into the toilet or simply standing there?
I hold my breath, waiting for the flush.
At last it comes; you return to bed.

But now the sheets are choking me.
I'm nightmare warm, hot flashing,
all the memory of your illness
flooding past my broken dam of dreams.
As the clock chimes 5 a.m.,
I shove my feet into fuzzy slippers,
grab glasses, robe and flashlight.
The dog lies tucked and silent, listening
as another Alzheimer's day begins.

DEMENTIA DIVORCE

I guess it's official.
I'm living in the guest room.
It happened gradually,
sneaking out at 2 a.m.
to escape his moans and flailing arms,
his conversations with people
who weren't there, the lights
I plugged in everywhere
to keep him from getting lost,
yet I still found him in the closet
looking for the bathroom door.

When the dog died, I gave up, too.
We both left my husband's room.
Last week, I moved my nightstand,
Grandma's lamp, my clock,
my handkerchiefs and rosaries,
leaving him the better mattress
while I slept on a pile of lumps.
Then yesterday, a rainy day,
I bounced from bed to bed
at the furniture store while he
stood sipping coffee, content,
as if I wasn't leaving him.

Today when the men arrived,
dark-haired, handsome Mexicans
who carried out my broken bed
and set up my new "pillowtop,"
I wondered if they wondered
why I looked so very sad.
Of course they didn't ask.
"Sign here, ma'am," they said.
Dripping tears, I made my bed
and lay on it, not quite sure,
left, right or dead center.
Does it matter anymore?

COFFEE STAINS

Oh, how tricky they think they are,
talking all around me about housework,
cooking some dinner, maybe taking me
to the grocery store, working on the honey-dos,
but they don't fool me any, those nice ladies
with their soft voices so sorry for the paperwork.

And my wife so eager yes, yes, oh yes
like she used to say in bed, or was that
just the whores in the dirty movies, I can't
remember. I touch her, she moves away.
"I'm tired, I'm sick, I'm stressed, I just can't
do it all," she says. "I need help," but she never

asks me to do anything except maybe get up,
get dressed, what do you want to eat,
did you remember to take your pills? I
could clean the God-damned house or she
could quit her piddling jobs and let me be
the man of the house. I'm not dead yet.

Oh boy, watch her filling out those forms as if
I can't even remember my given name. Well, I don't
actually know what day it is or who these ladies
are, but so what? I haven't lost my mind, no sir.
Wait, is someone coming to drive me away?
What did I do? What did she just say? Okay?

"Would you like more coffee?" I ask.
Just for an instant, the talking stops.
All the women stare at me. The brunette--
Leslie?--smiles, says, "Thank you, yes I would."
But as soon as my back is turned, I hear
her click her pen and make a note.

Does the red light mean it's on or off?
I hate this Mr. Coffee pot.
Never mind. I'll pull the plug.
Damn! I missed the lady's cup.
My wife snatches the pot away from me
as java spreads across the tablecloth.

VISION

My father's mind is fading.
I just found him in the street
behind my favorite bistro.

He stared at me, confused,
light gone from his eyes,
suddenly so old, so bent.

In that moment, I could see
what he saw, a tall stranger,
leather-clad, tattooed.

"Hey Dad," I said, trying
to laugh, but my voice
came out like sobs.

My stepmom led him home
while I stayed at the bar,
my glasses on the table,

drinking myself blind.

WHAT A FEELING

When I first saw your penis,
we lay kissing on the floor,
yellow blanket on a braided rug,
"Flashdance" on the video screen,
orange flame in the fireplace.

Lord, it was big. Would it fit?
No, but I welcomed the pain,
the tearing me open. Come in,
come in, and fill every inch.
"What a Feeling." That was the song.

A life of loving later,
on a matted magenta rug,
you lie beside the piano leg
while I'm dialing nine one one.
Spaghetti boils over on the stove.

You say you need to pee.
As I hold your penis gingerly
over aging Tupperware,
it's small and soft as a baby's.
Your urine smells like rotten fruit.

In your narrow hospital bed,
you keep tearing off your gown,
catheter stabbed into the hole,
piss flowing down a plastic tube
to a bag marked off with liter lines.

To the nurses passing by, it's just
another wrinkled body part
like an elbow or a nose,
exposed and rendered meaningless,
but I still feel it down below.

GRAVEL ROAD AHEAD

Where my husband lives now,
I don't. Each day he forgets more
details from the house we bought
with his VA loan. I don't. I tend them,
sort his papers, pay his bills,
dust his antique rolltop desk.

I linger in his swivel chair,
wearing his red plaid shirt, staring
at my small hands peeking out
from frayed cuffs with missing buttons,
toying with his ballpoint pen.

I straighten his paper clips, delaying
my drive up the steep winding road
to where my husband lives now
in a numbered room with an ocean view,
where the pavement ends, and I don't.

NOT STAYING

Up on the hill where everyone has wheelchairs,
I hurry in on two good feet, "not staying"
written on my face. I say hello to Pat,
nod at deafened Charlie, skirt the gal
who runs the place and always wants to talk
about how "he's getting worse, I think."
Well, yes, that's why he's here.

His name's up on the door. I push,
never knowing what I'll find: Will he be
doing nothing, greeting me in tears, or
pointing at his razor? "I don't like this one."
Fine. I'll buy another one. And another pack
of diapers, too. I'll order him more pills.
Meanwhile, we sit down to chat,
but there's nothing left to say.

He can't remember breakfast, doesn't
know who came or went. He says,
"How's everyone at home?" when
"everyone's" just me. He asks again
when he can leave. I tell him
I don't know. We might go out
for a walk or watch a TV show.
Then I hear the meal cart. Praise God.

It's time for me to go.
We kiss. He weeps. I flee.

FRIDAY AFTERNOON

Behind the nursing home,
the grass rolls lush and steep
to greenhouses and gardens,
a red barn, a farmhouse.
Far below, the ocean
sparkles blue and silver
in pale April sun.

I lead him down the driveway,
stumbling and shuffling,
his footsteps off the beat.
I hold his boneless hand,
urge him to sit on the lawn.
As sunlight burns our cheeks,
he begins to shake, to weep.

Beauty brings no comfort,
not green, not red, not blue,
not gold upon our skin.
"When can I go home?" he asks.
I kiss his bristly cheeks,
match our wedding bands.
A robin sings nearby.

WIFELY DUTY

All the years of our marriage,
I would not touch his feet.
His jagged toenails stuck out,
sharp, yellow, fungus-crumbled.
I loved his face, his ears,
his penis. I would count the moles
on his strong, speckled back,
kiss his sweaty bald spot.
But never an arch, a heel, a toe.

Today at the nursing home,
I pulled off his smelly socks
and faced the ugly aged feet.
I rubbed his flaky dried-out
heels with thick sticky cream,
stroked his purpled insteps,
caressed his puffy arches.
I massaged each gnarled toe,
tenderly so as not to hurt.

But Lord Jesus, who washed
the twelve apostles' feet
full of blisters, boils, and dirt,
then forgave them all their sins,
forgive me my squeamishness.
I left my husband barefoot
staring at his naked feet,
wondering who I was
as I ran to wash my hands.

JUST ANOTHER DAY

I pull boxer shorts from my bag,
rip open the plastic, get busy
writing Room 107 in the waistbands,
put them folded in your drawer.

"Our anniversary is coming," I say.
"How many?" You've lost the word "years."
"Twenty-five." I thirst for champagne
sipped from crystal goblets.

"Will I be there?" you ask. Oh, love.
Do you remember holding hands atop
white candlelit tablecloths, sharing bites
of chocolate cake, licking each other's lips?

You fiddle with your pants, get up.
"I have to pee." You run away.
I gaze outside as winter rain
streaks the glass with icy tears.

ALZHEIMER'S ACTIVITY

When a yellow balloon
drifts their way,
they stretch aged hands
to pat it, bop it, slug it,
laughing as it hits the lamp
or grazes a lady's hair.
Eyes bright, they catch it,
amazed, then send it off,
a bubble in the air.

Frank with one front tooth
leans forward in his chair,
gives it a good whack.
It bounces off Jimmy's shoe.
He kicks it up to the couch.
Fred butts it with his head,
Merritt taps it, ladylike,
Jean, purple bracelets clanging,
captures it and won't let go.
Forgetting the game, the players doze.

MEMORY CARE

The aides serve ice cream every day, and every day,
the residents are surprised at this new treat.
Handed bowls of vanilla scooped from tubs,
they stare at the white mounds floating there.
Some poke it with dirty fingers, spilling
ice cream over the sides, while others bend
and lick it like a cat. Some just set it down.
One man, we'll call him Frank, with just one tooth,
grabs a handful, makes a snowball, and throws it
at the TV set, where it slithers down the screen
over Hoss on the old Bonanza show.
"Bingo!" cries an old lady with an ice cream mustache.

THIS, TOO, WILL PASS AWAY

Hugging among the picture books
and giant purple rubber balls,
we clutch and kiss like teens,
fingers in each other's belts,
blind to the world around.

Arm in arm, we stroll
as they watch, heads hanging,
diapers dimpling stretch pants,
sitting in the dining room
at 2:30 waiting for supper.

He takes me to his room,
shows me his toothpaste,
his shoes, his dirty clothes,
his radio that doesn't work.
I turn the static into songs.

Sitting in swivel easy chairs,
he strokes my smooth brown hand
with his jagged-nailed thumb.
He tries to talk, but words,
words vanish like fireflies.

Wet-eyed, he whispers,
"I love you." I lean over
to kiss his bristly cheeks.
"I love you, too. So much."
He smiles. Sinatra sings.

EMPTY POCKETS

He's wearing somebody else's jeans.
They appeared in his closet, like
the khaki coat and blue socks,
shirts of every color. Now they're his,
making up for his missing underpants,
black socks, and coffee-stained slippers.

His pockets are empty. A man
with no memory has nothing to lose:
no wallet, no credit cards, no keys,
not even a wrinkled handkerchief.

He complains about these pants.
He unbuckles them, exposes himself
in front of the open window,
yanks out the flat pockets,
but now he can't remember why.

Once so shy, he doesn't notice
he's showing his dusky, white-haired
genitalia. Fresh-faced aides see them
every day. It doesn't matter anymore
whose pants he's wearing.

Soon enough, he'll pass them on.

LOVE REMAINS

I kiss you
when your mouth
tastes like ice cream
or spoiled eggs,
when your stubble
bites my lips
and you stink
of sweat and pee,
when you wear
your shirt backwards,
your jeans unzipped,
when your hands shake,
your words get stuck,
and you don't know
who I am--because
you do know
I'm the one
you kiss.

I'M YOUR WIFE

Sun shines in my eyes
as we rock in your mother's
mauve chairs in Room 107
at the memory care home.

My chair squeaks. Mental note:
bring WD-40. And diapers.
"Michael called," I say.
"Who's Michael?"

"Your son." Damn.
"Did you get a haircut?"
You reach up to feel.
"Yes. No. I don't know."

I wonder if you realize
that I'm your wife,
that my name is Sue,
that I don't work here.

Think of something to say.
"This giant dog jumps on my lap.
Then she licks my face like this."
I wiggle my tongue. You laugh.

"How many dogs do you have?"
I stare at a hood-jacketed teen
loping down the street.
She used to be *your* dog, too.

"One. It's just Annie and me."
I touch the gnarled vein
on your age-freckled hand.
You pull your hand away.

In the silence, the clock
chunks away the seconds.
You catch me looking.
"Well, thanks for coming."

You don't know who I am.

HE'LL NEVER KNOW

Today I threw his shoes away.
They were tan loafers, scuffed on the sides,
cracked around the heels. I can see them
on his feet with sweaty white socks.
Now I see his legs, in Levi's,
bowed like a boy's as he walks,
shoulders back, head up, always
a soldier. Now he's an old man
in a nursing home. He wears slippers,
he shuffles, he stares at the floor.

It was cold in his closet. His tweed jacket
caressed my hair as I crouched below,
seeking the source of the smell.
Brown suede hiking boots crusted with dirt,
black shoes shined up for church,
and in the back, the loafers, his favorites,
speckled with olive-green mold.
I two-fingered them into the trash
where they sank into used Kleenex,
carrot peels and coffee grounds.

KEEPING THE WIDOW WARM

"It's up to you now,"
says the pellet stove man,
pity in his watery eyes.

He shows me how to scrape,
brush, and suck the ash
to keep the fire hot.

"I'm so sorry," he says.
As they all do. Everyone.
"It's a hell of a thing."

He wants details about
my husband's Alzheimer's,
how he came to move away.

Hours and hours he works,
cursing, bleeding from cuts,
to make the stove perfect for me.

Pellets shoot down the slide
into the yellow-orange fire.
Grateful, I warm my hands.

Due to my in-between state,
a woman bereaved but not quite,
he gives me a "break" on the bill.

$740 and a free bottle
of Creosote Destroyer.
I guess this is how it will be.

Pellets sizzle down
into the yellow-orange fire
so hot it's burning my legs.

NEW YEAR'S DAY, ALBANY GENERAL, ROOM 204

Your trembling hand reaches for mine
across the rail of a hospital bed.

Downy gray hair splays across the pillow,
smooth white skin under overgrown beard.

Cotton gown slips from hairy shoulders,
rides up, exposing a wrinkled blue diaper.

Animal sounds, words that aren't words,
maybe curses, are all you have left.

I spoon applesauce onto your fleshy tongue,
feed you French fries, coffee through a straw.

Urine flows yellow down a rubber tube
into a half-full plastic bag.

Pony-tailed nurse with stutter speech
straightens your sheets, checks your heart.

Indian doctor says to let you go.
Your legs twitch, you make motorboat sounds.

I sit for hours, my head in my hands,
peeking through my fingers, watching you breathe.

Last night, New Year's Eve, you
left without saying goodbye. Now,

as the Rose Bowl flickers on a muted TV,
I'm hungry, but I will not leave while

your trembling hand reaches for mine
across the rail of the hospital bed.

YOUR KISS IN THE BACK OF A BUICK

I watched them place your ashes
in a cemetery niche. I have sat
crying amid the stink of dying flowers
beneath the black urn like a vase
with no opening, your name etched in gold,
a name I never called you. No.
I know you're not inside that urn.

Tonight, riding in a car, full moon
following as we passed fields
where cows dozed beneath the stars,
I remembered your kisses. I felt
your lips on mine, warm,
pressing hard, your playful tongue,
and I knew that you were here,
here in the dark back seat
of my sister-in-law's Buick.
Green lights on the dashboard,
long black road ahead,
my niece and nephew close,
I felt you hold my hand.
I heard you speak my name.

In that cold room in the daylight,
where I come to change your flowers,
I can't find you in the cubbyhole
with your mom and dad nearby.
When I speak, I hear only echoes
as I shed my widow's tears.
No, you're right here in my arms.

HIS WHISKER

I found one of his whiskers.
Oh, how I used to curse them
littering the sink
after he trimmed his mustache,
piercing my lips when we kissed,
but now this last one
from the crease of a book
rests atop my fingertip
like a fallen eyelash.
I don't know whether
to save it in a box
or make a wish
and blow it away.

WIDOW ON THE ROAD

Above the roaring fan, she hears
a roar that could be a car
warming up in the motel lot,
a hair dryer or the ice machine,
but no, it's snoring behind the wall.
The wild-haired tattooed trucker
is "sawing logs" in his sleep.
Alone in her rented bed,
she smiles, settles into her pillow
and matches her breath to his.

SISTER ALZHEIMER'S WIFE

Sister Alzheimer's wife, I know you,
even though we have never met.
I know the fear every time he
forgets something he used to know
like how to make a sandwich
or where the salad dressing goes.

I know you lie awake at night
watching him hallucinate,
fighting monsters in the bed
or not remembering who you are.
He gets lost and pees on the rug.
You're so tired you want to run away.

I know you weep where he cannot hear,
in the car, the garage, on the toilet seat,
then hurry to answer his calls for help—
turn on the TV or button his shirt—
while the house needs work, lawns aren't mowed,
and the oil light's been on in the car for weeks.

I know you watch the money go
as you pay bills you never paid before—
doctors, car repair, and soon the nursing home.
Married but not a wife anymore,
you miss kissing and sex and wine-soaked talks
sharing memories only you remember now.

Oh sister, I know you feel alone,
that no one understands the way it is,
that he's disappearing bit by bit, even
if he looks the same as he always did,
and it's not fair, not fair, not f-ing fair.
But you promised, so you stay.

Oh sister Alzheimer's wife, I know.
I rode that ride from beginning to end,
plastered in place by centrifugal force,
till it stopped and I wobbled off alone,
dizzy and sick to my stomach, yes,
but I staggered on. And so will you.

Sue Fagalde Lick spent many years working as a journalist in California's Bay Area before relocating with her late husband to the Oregon coast. In the middle of their journey through Alzheimer's Disease, she earned her MFA at Antioch University Los Angeles and turned her attention to poetry and creative nonfiction. Her work has appeared in *Rattle, The MacGuffin, Willawa, Creative Nonfiction, Persimmon Tree, New Letters, The American Journal of Poetry*, and other publications. She also blogs at *www.unleashedinoregon.com* and *www.childlessbymarriage.com*. Her books include *Stories Grandma Never Told: Portuguese Women in California, Childless by Marriage*, and *Up Beaver Creek*. When not writing, she switches hats, puts away her swear words, and goes to work as a music minister at Sacred Heart Church in Newport, Oregon.

www.ingramcontent.com/pod-product-compliance
Lightning Source LLC
LaVergne TN
LVHW041506070426
835507LV00012B/1374